BE YOUR OWN
LAWN EXPERT

BY DR. D. G. HESSAYON

2nd EDITION
of Britain's best-selling
book on lawn care

2/6

Contents

1st EDITION 600,000   2nd EDITION 1st impression 300,000
                                         2nd impression 250,000

COMPANION VOLUMES in the same series

BE YOUR OWN
GARDENING EXPERT
1st EDITION 1,600,000

BE YOUR OWN
ROSE EXPERT
1st EDITION 1,100,000

BE YOUR OWN
HOUSE PLANT EXPERT
1st EDITION   800,000
2nd EDITION 1,000,000

 PUBLISHED BY PAN BRITANNICA INDUSTRIES LTD., WALTHAM CROSS, HERTS., ENGLAND.

CHAPTER 1
LOOKING AT YOUR LAWN

The lawn is the backcloth which sets the scene in your garden. In summer, it unites bright and varied bits of scenery. In winter its role is reversed; it brings greenness and life to an empty stage.

Every gardener realises this and wants a first rate lawn. The purpose of this book is to show how it can be achieved. The first step is to learn to recognise a good lawn when you see one. . . .

How to recognise LAWN TYPES

Walk slowly over the turf and examine it carefully.
Then answer the following questions—

TICK IF THE ANSWER IS YES

1.	Is the surface free from bumps and depressions?
2.	Is it the same green colour and even texture all over?
3.	Is it practically free from weeds?
4.	Is it free from small heaps of earth and bare patches?
5.	Is it reasonably quick-draining after heavy rain?
6.	Is it free from brown patches?

Six ticks indicate a first rate lawn. It may be

FIRST RATE LAWN: Luxury grade   or   **FIRST RATE LAWN: Utility grade**

See pages 4-5 for details of the difference between them.
If your score is less than six ticks, answer questions 7 and 8 —

7.	Is it full of weeds and/or moss, with very little grass present? Do not mistake Pearlwort for grass—see page 22 for recognition.
8.	Is it very thin, made up of coarse grass and weeds, with bare earth showing through everywhere?

If you have marked no ticks to these two questions, then you have a **SECOND RATE LAWN** (see page 6).

If you have ticked one of these questions, then you have a **WORN OUT LAWN** (see page 6).

How to recognise GOOD DESIGN

A square or rectangle is the most labour-saving shape, but a simple, irregular outline is felt by many people to be more attractive. Avoid small and fussy curves at all costs.

The lawn need not be horizontal; a gentle slope of about 1 in 80 is quite satisfactory. But the surface should be level; bumps and hollows must be avoided. Ideally the site should be completely unshaded. It should not be in dense shade or troubles will arise.

A lawn constructed under the branches of trees will be difficult or impossible to maintain in good condition.

most popular lawn size in Britain is 1,000 sq. ft.

Flower beds are best left out of the lawn. If included they should be restricted to one or two, with simple shapes and proportions in keeping with the size of the lawn.

It should be possible to mow right along the edge of the lawn, which means that the turf should not extend to the base of walls, fences or raised paths.
Avoid grass banks if possible. Verges should be at least 30 inches wide.

Paths should not lead directly on to the grass, but should run along one side of the lawn.

THE FIRST RATE LAWN : Luxury Grade

There is no mistaking the luxury grade of turf. Its velvety close pile has the typical "bowling green" look, and this is *the* turf for the ornamental lawn.

If you want your lawn to be a thing of beauty, with its main function being to arouse the envy of friends and neighbours, then you must aim for this grade of turf. But be warned, there are a number of drawbacks and difficulties which you must face up to from the start.

- Luxury grasses will not stand up to very hard wear, such as the busy feet of children at play.
- Luxury grasses will not stand neglect in the same way as the utility grade, so be prepared for a regular routine of lawn management.
- Seed and turf are expensive.
- Establishment of the new luxury lawn is a long process, as the grasses concerned are slow growing.
- Careful site preparation before seeding or turfing is all-important as any coarse grass left in the soil will quickly ruin the "bowling green" effect.

Luxury grasses

Luxury turf consists entirely of fine-leaved dwarf grasses. Perennial Ryegrass and the other coarser lawn grasses are absent.

BENTS (Agrostis species)

BROWNTOP
(Agrostis tenuis)

The commonest Bent of all —present to some extent in all lawns.

Creeping, with short runners.

Tough, permanent and drought-resistant.

bottom of the leaf blade

CREEPING BENT
(Agrostis stolonifera)

Becoming more common with the increase in popularity of the "planted" lawn.

Creeping, with above-ground runners.

Spreads quickly, but does not stand up well to hard wear.

VELVET BENT
(Agrostis canina)

Grows well on dry soils.

Similar to Creeping Bent, but spreads more slowly and the leaves are much finer.

FESCUES (Festuca species)

CHEWINGS FESCUE
(Festuca rubra fallax)

Popular grass in luxury turf mixes.

Does not creep; grows in tufts.

Sometimes pushed out by the more aggressive Bent grasses.

Drought-resistant, dark green.

CREEPING RED FESCUE
(Festuca rubra genuina)

Popular grass in luxury turf mixes.

Creeping, with under-ground stems.

SHEEP'S FESCUE
(Festuca ovina)

Grows wild on heaths and downs.

Does not creep; grows in distinct tufts. Does not blend well with other grasses.

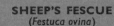

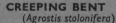

THE FIRST RATE LAWN: Utility Grade

A lawn in which Perennial Ryegrass and other broad-leaved turf grasses are dominant does not compare in beauty with the luxury Bent/Fescue lawn. However, if time and money are limited, and the lawn is designed to be useful rather than ornamental, then the utility lawn is the one to choose.

Perennial Ryegrass has, a little undeservedly, a bad reputation. This is mainly due to the rather poor nature of the ordinary strains which are sometimes used in seed mixtures. It is true that this grass is a weed in the luxury lawn, but the modern leafy varieties, such as S.23 and Kentish Indigenous, successfully form the basis of a first rate utility lawn.

The drawback of this type of lawn is that the grass grows more quickly and so regular and frequent mowing is essential. Also the velvet look is missing.

On the credit side, seed and turf are cheap and the new lawn establishes itself rapidly. The grass will stand neglect to a remarkable extent and the natural coarse grasses which appear are nearly always hidden.

Utility grasses

Fine-leaved grasses, such as Bents and Fescues, should be present with one or more of the following coarser species in order to make up a thick, closely knit turf.

PERENNIAL RYEGRASS
(Lolium perenne)

bottom of the leaf blade

Very common in utility lawns. Suitable for heavy soils.

Extremely hard-wearing, but will not stand very close mowing.

Does not creep; grows in tufts.

Leaves shiny underneath, with distinctive "ears". Leaf bases usually pink.

CRESTED DOG'S-TAIL
(Cynosurus cristatus)

Grows wild on heaths. Suitable for dry soils.

Extremely hard-wearing. Withstands drought.

Does not creep; grows in tufts.

Very similar to Perennial Ryegrass but leaves do not have "ears" and the leaf bases are not pink.

ROUGH-STALKED MEADOW GRASS
(Poa trivialis)

Valuable for moist, heavy soils and shady sites.

Does not stand up well to hard wear.

Creeping, with above-ground runners.

SMOOTH-STALKED MEADOW GRASS
(Poa pratensis)

The Kentucky Bluegrass of North America.

Valuable for light soils as it is drought-resistant. Hard-wearing.

Creeping, with under-ground stems.

ANNUAL MEADOW GRASS
(Poa annua)

Extremely common in all lawns.

Usually regarded as a weed, but in difficult situations such as under trees it forms a useful turf.

TIMOTHY
(Phleum pratense)

Useful for moist, heavy soils.

Stands up to hard wear but cannot tolerate close mowing.

Creeping, with above-ground runners.

THE SECOND RATE LAWN

In this type of lawn one or more of the common troubles illustrated on page 15 are present, but there is still a reasonable covering of desirable turf grasses.

To many gardeners, the lawn is merely something which has to be kept down by mowing when it gets untidy. But even the perfect lawn gets out of condition if neglected or subjected to incorrect treatment for only a short time. This is because turf grasses have their own special needs, which must be catered for by regular feeding, top dressing, aerating, and weeding. It is therefore not surprising that the great majority of lawns in this country are second rate.

The cure . . . .

The second rate lawn can be brought back in to first rate condition because the essential ingredient, a good distribution of turf grasses, is still present.

The first step is to think carefully about the cause of the deterioration. What went wrong? The table in the next column and the chapter on Lawn Troubles will help you to identify the faults and understand their cure.

Next, apply the remedy. This may be a simple treatment in the case of a single fault, such as earthworm activity. On the other hand it may be a lengthy process if the lawn has been neglected for some time and has a varied collection of lawn complaints. In this case the renovation routine on page 25 should be followed.

Finally, having brought the lawn back into its first rate state, keep it there by proper management. This does not mean a buying spree for expensive equipment and chemicals. Nor does it entail constant hard work and drudgery. Its price is an understanding of the needs of turf grasses, and the application of this knowledge as a *regular* routine.

Lawn care becomes back-breaking only when things are allowed to get out of hand.

. . . . and the cause

1. **POOR CONSTRUCTION.** When making a new lawn, careful attention must be paid to site preparation, drainage and the selection of turf or seed. Carelessness here is likely to lead to poor quality turf.

2. **NEGLECT.** This is generally due to ignorance of the needs of a lawn:

Neglected mowing means cutting the grass only when it is overgrown and looks untidy. Over-close irregular shaving is one of the commonest causes of lawn destruction.

Neglected feeding means that the grasses do not have the strength to produce a vigorous thick turf. Moss is a symptom here.

Neglected aeration of the surface means that the roots are starved of air.

Neglected weeding means that a simple five-minute job develops into an almost insuperable task.

3. **INCORRECT TREATMENT.** Too much of the wrong treatment is as harmful as too little of the right one. Liming when it isn't necessary, too much fertiliser in the autumn, frequent use of a heavy roller—all can ruin good grass.

A badly set or blunt mower can do a great deal of harm, as it mutilates instead of cutting the grass cleanly.

4. **THE UNAVOIDABLES.** Smoke and grime in cities, heavy shade, the drip from overhanging trees, the busy feet of children and the urine of female dogs are all serious problems which are not due to either the laziness or thoughtlessness of the gardener.

THE WORN OUT LAWN

This is easily distinguished from the other types, because here the lawn grasses have practically or entirely disappeared. Their place has been taken by moss, broad-leaved weeds, weed grasses or bare earth.

Many green and superficially acceptable lawns are, on close inspection, found to be made up entirely of moss and pearlwort.

The use of a weedkiller in these cases is most unwise. This would result in the burning-off of the whole surface, and the eventual recolonisation by another horde of weeds.

If it is decided that the lawn must be brought back to its former grassy self, then the only thing to do is to clear away the surface and start again, following the rules for the creation of a new lawn.

LAWN CARE

A lawn to be proud of . . . .

This wish of all gardeners is quite easily satisfied if a number of simple and straightforward tasks are tackled as a regular routine and not as cures each time the signs of neglect appear.

The first task is to collect together the right tools for the job.

ESSENTIALS

Equipment

Mower. The most important item, of course!

Fertiliser spreader. Essential for the even application of lawn dressing over large areas.

Besom or birch broom. Costs only a few shillings, but is invaluable for sweeping up leaves and dispersing worm casts. Occasional brushing during the season encourages the fine grasses.

Garden fork. The easiest way of deeply aerating the turf.

Edging shears. Essential for trimming the edges after mowing. Ordinary hand shears make this a back-breaking job unless the lawn is small.

Wire rake. or 'Springbok'. Essential for scarifying the turf. Has a tonic effect by breaking up the surface "mat".

Hose and sprinkler. Essential in a dry summer.

Sieve ($\frac{1}{4}$ inch mesh). Essential for preparing top dressings.

USEFUL ADDITIONS

Half-moon edging iron. Useful for obtaining a neat edge at the start of the season, but it must not be used too often.

Lawn sweeper. Saves a lot of time, in the autumn on the large lawn, as it collects leaves and rubbish quickly and easily.

Spiked roller. Useful for scarifying large areas.

Hollow tine fork. Useful for improving the drainage of lawns on heavy soil.

Light roller (not more than 2 cwt.) For use in the spring after frost.

Watering can. Very useful for the application of weedkillers, etc.

Metal edging. Stops grass spreading into flower beds and keeps the edges firm at all times.

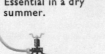

Fertilisers & Chemicals

In the spring Grass-greening **Fertiliser rich in nitrogen** and a **Hormone Weedkiller** are the main needs. A combined treatment (e.g. Toplawn) saves time and money.

Lawn Sand is a tonic/weedkiller which also checks moss. **Spot Weedkiller** eradicates isolated weeds. **Calomel Dust** is the standard moss killer.

In the autumn **Top Dressings** (page 14) and **Complete Fertiliser** to build up the root system for next year. **Derris** checks worms and **Quintozene** prevents Fusarium disease. A combined treatment (Autumn Toplawn) is available.

LAWN CARE BY MOWING

"*Country gentlemen will find in using my machine an amusing, useful and healthful exercise. . . .*"
Original cylinder mower patent issued to Edwin Budding 1830.

The purpose of mowing is not merely to keep down unsightly growth. When correctly carried out, it builds up a vigorous, fine quality grass sward. The secret is to **keep the grass long enough to prevent the roots being starved, but short enough to be attractive to the onlooker. This height must not vary a great deal during the growing season.**

The rule is to mow often, but not too closely. In this way excess leaf-growth is prevented, fertiliser loss curtailed, and the menace of weeds, worms and coarse grasses reduced. The grass itself assumes a dwarf habit and the production of extra shoots is stimulated.

Close shaving at irregular intervals is unfortunately an all-too-common practice. It means certain destruction of the good quality lawn, because the desirable grasses are rapidly weakened. The thin open turf which results is soon invaded by moss, pearlwort, annual meadow grass, daisies and yarrow.

The mower

The best machine for your lawn is one large enough to tackle the job comfortably, but small enough to fit in with your budget. The following notes will help you to make the right choice.

SIZE

A 12–14 inch cutting cylinder is the best size for the average lawn.

NUMBER OF BLADES

5–6 blades are usual on inexpensive machines for utility grade lawns.
8–10 blades are found on more expensive machines. Needed for fine finish on luxury grade turf.

TYPES OF MOWER

Side wheel models

The main advantage is that they are cheaper than the corresponding roller types. Another point in their favour is that they are better for cutting new lawns, and the absence of a front roller means better control of creeping weeds.

Roller models

The main advantage is that they can be used for cutting right up to the lawn edge. Another point in their favour is that the back roller gives a better finish. The best type to buy for the average lawn.

Rotary models

Power-driven rotary lawn mowers are useful where a very close cut is not required. A point in their favour is that tough-stalked grasses and weeds are not able to escape cutting, as sometimes happens with other types of mower.

Motor models

The petrol-driven, electric and battery machines undoubtedly take the backache out of lawn mowing. A motor mower is essential for the large lawn. For areas of less than 150 square yards they are hardly time saving. Also, the finish is no better than with a well-set hand machine.

Airborne models

The latest introduction is the 'hovercraft' type of machine which floats on a cushion of air and so is light and easy to handle. Cutting action and quality is similar to that of other rotary types of mower.

HEIGHT OF CUT

DANGER Course grasses start to swamp fine grasses — $1\frac{1}{2}$ inch

Utility lawn in spring, autumn or drought — $1\frac{1}{4}$ inch

Utility lawn in summer — 1 inch

Luxury lawn in spring, autumn or drought — $\frac{3}{4}$ inch

Luxury lawn in summer — $\frac{1}{2}$ inch

DANGER Strength of grass reduced — $\frac{1}{4}$ inch

WHEN TO CUT

Begin in March. Finish in October, apart from occasional light 'topping' in early winter when weather is mild.

Cut **twice a week** when the grass is growing vigorously in summer.

Cut **once a week** in spring, autumn and under drought conditions.

Cutting less than once a week when the grass is actively growing results in the sudden loss of a large quantity of leaf. This "shocks" the grass and reduces its vigour.

Before mowing

Raking should be carried out at about monthly intervals during the growing season. It is a valuable treatment before mowing because it sets up the grass and creeping weeds to meet the mower blades. Also, it opens up the surface "mat" of dead vegetation.

Brushing with a birch broom is a useful pre-mowing treatment when the grass is wet with dew or rain. If the drops of water on the leaves are not brushed off, mowing will result in serious bruising of the grass and the possibility of a "washboard" effect (see page 15).

Where worm casts are present on the lawn, these must be scattered by brushing prior to mowing, or the surface will be spoilt.

When mowing

To cut down the risk of "skinning" the high spots, the mower should be pushed **forward**. A heavy downward pressure should be avoided.

Cutting the grass by a series of backward-and-forward pushing motions is not good practice. The correct technique is to work in a constant forward direction at a steady walking pace.

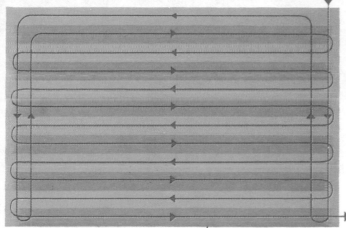

The way to obtain 'Zebra stripes'

Alternate light and dark bands on a mown lawn are taken by many people to be a sign of quality. They are nothing of the sort, of course; they are merely the result of the lawn being cut in parallel strips, alternate strips being mown in opposite directions.

A much more important routine is to cut at right angles to the line of the previous mowing. If the work has been carried out in a north-south line, then the next cutting should be in an east-west direction. This cross-cutting keeps down the coarse weed grasses and stops "washboarding" (see page 15).

After mowing

Clippings, caked mud, etc., should be brushed off the rollers and cutting cylinder. Wipe over with an oily rag.

The moving parts of the machine need oiling regularly, as directed in the instruction manual. An annual overhaul is usually advisable, and this is best left to the local agent. Have the work done during the winter; do not wait until the grass has started to grow in the spring!

Using the grass box

Under normal conditions, the grass-box should be fitted and the clippings used for compost-making or mulching.

If clippings are regularly left on the surface in damp weather, then the production of casts by earthworms will become a serious problem.

The box can be left off when mowing during a dry spell in summer provided that daisies or annual meadow grass are not a problem.

LAWN CARE BY SPIKING

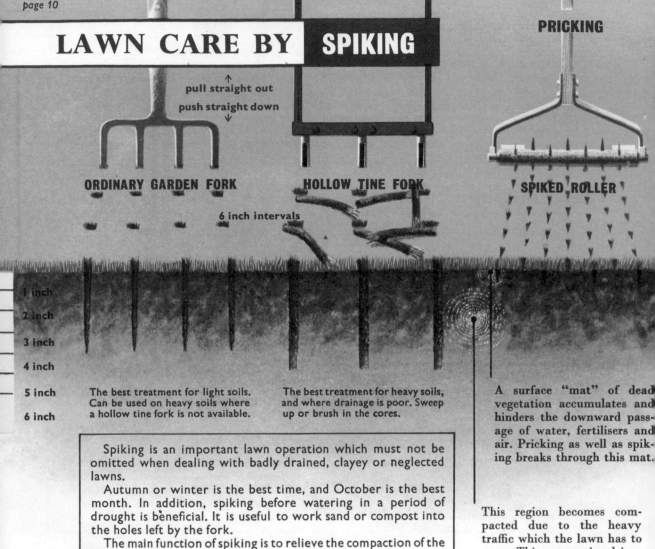

PRICKING

pull straight out
push straight down

ORDINARY GARDEN FORK

HOLLOW TINE FORK

SPIKED ROLLER

6 inch intervals

1 inch
2 inch
3 inch
4 inch
5 inch
6 inch

The best treatment for light soils. Can be used on heavy soils where a hollow tine fork is not available.

The best treatment for heavy soils, and where drainage is poor. Sweep up or brush in the cores.

A surface "mat" of dead vegetation accumulates and hinders the downward passage of water, fertilisers and air. Pricking as well as spiking breaks through this mat.

Spiking is an important lawn operation which must not be omitted when dealing with badly drained, clayey or neglected lawns.

Autumn or winter is the best time, and October is the best month. In addition, spiking before watering in a period of drought is beneficial. It is useful to work sand or compost into the holes left by the fork.

The main function of spiking is to relieve the compaction of the sub-surface layer. The air channels treated in this region improve the drainage and the growth of new roots is greatly stimulated. These roots render the lawn more resistant to drought during the following summer.

This region becomes compacted due to the heavy traffic which the lawn has to carry. This compaction drives out air, and root development becomes stifled. Spiking, but not pricking, penetrates this zone.

LAWN CARE BY ROLLING

The faulty use of a garden roller is a common cause of lawn deterioration. In the hands of the skilled professional greenkeeper the roller does useful work by consolidating the surface and producing an attractive "face". But for the ordinary gardener normal treading and the weight of a roller mower are generally all that is required to consolidate the surface of a lawn on heavy or loamy soil.

Only in the spring does the roller have an important function on established turf. It should not weigh more than 2 cwt. and it should be used only when the surface is dry and when the soil below is damp. Brush off worm casts, surface debris, etc., before rolling. The purpose of this early spring rolling is to reconsolidate the turf which has been lifted by frost.

Never roll when the grass is wet or thin and do not attempt to level out bumps in this way.

LAWN CARE BY WATERING

Grass cannot live without water. The amount of rainfall in this country is usually sufficient to keep the roots well supplied with moisture. But prolonged dry spells do occasionally occur in late spring and summer, and the need for extra water arises.

THE PROBLEM

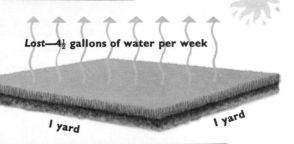

Lost—4½ gallons of water per week

1 yard   1 yard

On the established lawn, the leaves start to turn brown and die as soon as the top 4 inches have dried out. No amount of fertiliser can stop this effect.

If water, in the form of rain or artificial watering is still not forthcoming, then the crowns and roots of the grasses also die.

Certain weeds, notably clover, are drought-resistant and so are able to spread rapidly under very dry conditions when the growth of grass is reduced or stopped.

TACKLING THE PROBLEM

1 Increase drought-resistance

All techniques which stimulate deep and vigorous root development build up the natural drought-resistance of the grass. Autumn spiking, regular but not overkeen mowing, top-dressing and careful feeding all contribute towards this end.

If bulky organic material and horticultural vermiculite such as Veri-gro are incorporated into the soil of a lawn under construction, its water-holding capacity will be increased.

2 Carry out deep watering

The purpose of artificial watering is to refill the soil's reserve of water which has begun to run dry because of the warm dry weather. Watering must never be used merely to dampen the surface; this often does more harm than good.

WHEN?

The first sign of dryness is the loss of "springiness" in the grass. This is the best time to start.

The next stage in the effect of drought is a change in colour—the bright green goes and a grey-green hue appears.

Finally, the leaves yellow, turn brown and die. Browning of the grass is a sign that watering has been too long delayed. The roots are the last part of the plant to die.

Watering is usually carried out in the late afternoon or evening, but it will do no harm in bright sunshine in the middle of the day. Tests have also shown that, despite the popular fallacy, cold water is perfectly safe.

If the surface is compacted or contains a mat of dead vegetation, pricking or spiking before watering will aid penetration.

HOW?

Except for the really small lawn, a watering-can is useless. A hose fitted with a fine rose can be used, especially on sloping ground, but the best watering device of all is the revolving or oscillating sprinkler.

Perforated plastic tubing is quite popular, but the distribution of the spray is inferior to that of the sprinkler.

HOW MUCH?

The use of 5 or 6 "test-tins" (empty tin cans) will tell you the evenness of the distribution and the number of minutes the sprinkler should be run.

The ground should be soaked to a depth of at least 4 inches.

½ inch of water=2¼ gallons per square yard. This is the minimum which can be applied.

1 inch of water=4½ gallons per square yard. This is the amount needed to replace fully the water lost during a week of dry weather.

HOW OFTEN?

This will depend upon the soil type and the weather.

Lawns on sandy soil are more affected by drought than those on loamy or clayey soil, and so more frequent watering is necessary in light-land areas. The lawn should *partly* dry out between waterings. This lets in air and stimulates deep root formation. Under ordinary dry conditions this means watering once a week, and twice a week in hot, very dry weather.

Sprinkling every day or even every other day with small amounts of water is bad practice. This constant soaking of the surface leads to the spread of moss and pearlwort and the production of a shallow root system by the grasses.

LAWN CARE BY FEEDING

Why bother?

During late spring and summer, the rapid growth of grass means that frequent mowing is essential. A previous chapter pointed out the dangers if grass is allowed to grow too tall, so turf must be kept at the recommended height no matter how actively it is growing.

On this basis it might seem that feeding turf is a foolish thing to do. Isn't it hard enough to keep turf in check without forcing it to grow even more quickly?

The simple answer is that the plant foods contained in a compound lawn fertiliser do much more than make the grass grow quickly. Their main task is to produce **closely knit** turf in which neither moss nor weeds can obtain a ready foothold. The grass stays an attractive shade of green, and there is a build-up in the resistance to drought and disease.

Mowing is a serious drain on the soil's reserve of major plant foods. When nitrogen, phosphates and potash are in short supply, the lawn becomes thin and discoloured. **Good lawn management calls for a regular lawn feeding programme.**

The ingredients of a lawn feeding programme

	PLANT FOOD	USE ON THE LAWN	EFFECT	IMPORTANT SOURCES	BEST TIME TO APPLY
	NITROGEN greens grass makes the leaves grow faster	ESSENTIAL	Lush, green turf is produced when available nitrogen is present in the soil. Nitrogen in fertiliser may be immediately or only slowly available—wording on package should tell you which.	Spring and summer compound lawn fertiliser (e.g. Toplawn) Lawn sand (e.g. Velvas) Sulphate of ammonia	Spring and summer
	PHOSPHATES build up the root system	ESSENTIAL	A large root system is produced. This means that fresh reserves of food are tapped. The result is healthier grass and earlier growth in the spring.	Bone meal Autumn compound lawn fertiliser (e.g. Autumn Toplawn) Superphosphates	Autumn (Apply in spring if autumn application is missed)
	POTASH stimulates healthy growth	DESIRABLE	Not as vital as nitrogen or phosphates, but there is evidence that its use "hardens" the grass and so makes it less susceptible to drought, disease and discoloration.	Compound lawn fertiliser Sulphate of potash	Spring or autumn
	LIME	USE ONLY IN SPECIAL CASES	The only time to consider liming is when the grass is sparse and overrun by moss, woodrush and sheep's sorrel. In this case use 2 oz. ground limestone per sq. yd. The use of lime on an ordinary lawn will quite quickly lead to deterioration. As a general rule, try to keep your lawn acid by using peat and lawn sand and never using lime.	Hydrated garden lime Ground limestone	Autumn

Fertilisers and the weather

Before feeding

A spell of showery weather is best. Dry weather and drought should be avoided; if treatment must be done at such times, water thoroughly shortly before application.

When feeding

The grass leaves should be **dry** and the soil should be **moist** at the time of treatment.

After feeding

If rain does not fall for 2 days after application, water the treated lawn thoroughly to carry the fertiliser down into the soil.

THE LAWN FEEDING PROGRAMME

The newcomer to gardening can be excused for being confused. There are as many feeding programmes as there are books on lawn care. But this does not mean that the feeding of grass is a haphazard affair. All good schemes have the same fundamental foundation; it is only the less important details which differ.

PHOSPHATES are applied in autumn, to be present before growth starts.

NITROGEN enters the feeding story in spring, and it is usual to give the first dressing in the form of a compound fertiliser containing phosphates and a little potash in addition to nitrogen. Some proprietary brands contain both quick- and slow-acting nitrogen. "Toplawn", for instance, releases nitrogen over a period of months.

Summer feeding is necessary, but there is no general agreement on the form it should take. Some experts advise one or more dressings of sulphate of ammonia at $\frac{1}{2}$ oz. per square yard. Another way of obtaining a rapid green-up of tired summer turf is to apply a nitrogen-rich liquid feed such as pbi Lawn Tonic. Others feel that a second dressing of the compound fertiliser used in the spring is the best idea.

The 3 part plan

The plan below is an example of a balanced lawn-feeding programme. It incorporates all of the essential elements, and has the added benefit of dealing with weeds, worms and disease at the same time.

AUTUMN

Autumn Toplawn
at 2 oz. per 10 square feet.
ESSENTIAL

LATE SPRING

Toplawn
at 2 oz. per 10 square feet.
ESSENTIAL

SUMMER

Toplawn
at 2 oz. per 10 square feet.
DESIRABLE

FERTILISER APPLICATION

Whichever method of application is used, even distribution is essential or patchiness and perhaps scorch will be the result. Toplawn contains a special colourant to show you where you have been during application. When using materials which do not show up in this way, try to devise a way of marking to avoid overlapping or missed areas.

HAND APPLICATION   Hand application is still the most widely used method. If the fertiliser does not contain a weedkiller, it can be bulked up with four times its weight of sand or sieved soil. Apply half up and down the lawn, and then go back over the area crosswise with the remaining half.

LIQUID DILUTORS   The advantage of liquid fertilisers is that they are extremely quick-acting and not liable to scorch. The dilutor is filled with liquid fertiliser straight from the bottle and fitted to a garden hose. The correct dilution is obtained when the water is switched on. Bio Plant Food is suitable for this use.

MECHANICAL DISTRIBUTORS   These wheeled machines speed up fertiliser application, and can ensure more even results than by hand. However, if used carelessly a "tramline" effect is produced due to missed or double-dosed strips of turf. A hand-held distributor is now also available.

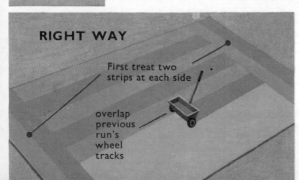

RIGHT WAY

First treat two strips at each side

overlap previous run's wheel tracks

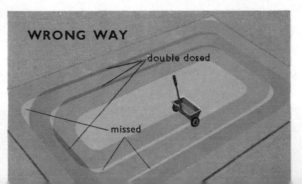

WRONG WAY

double dosed

missed

LAWN CARE BY TOP DRESSING

Top dressing means applying bulky materials which have very little or no fertiliser value.

It is one of the most important and yet least practised of all lawn care techniques. Everybody mows, the majority of lawn-owners weed, and a large number feed and water their turf. But only an enlightened few use a top dressing. For really first rate turf, you should top dress every year.

A made-to-measure top dressing for your lawn

- **PEAT.** Buy a fine-grade horticultural sphagnum peat, such as Irish Peat.

- **LOAM.** This is soil which is neither clayey nor sandy. The best loam is obtained from turves stacked grass-downwards until well rotted. Pass through a ¼ inch mesh sieve.

- **SAND.** Sea sand is not suitable as it must be lime-free.
  It has to be sharp river sand.

For lawns on heavy, clayey soil
- 1 part PEAT
- 2 parts LOAM
- 4 parts SAND

For lawns on loamy soil
- 1 part PEAT
- 4 parts LOAM
- 2 parts SAND

For lawns on light, sandy soil
- 2 parts PEAT
- 4 parts LOAM
- 1 part SAND

The dry ingredients should be mixed thoroughly before use.

How to use the top dressing

The best time is in the autumn. Spiking a day or two beforehand will greatly increase the benefits obtained.

Use 2 lb. per square yard, and spread evenly over the surface.

Work it well into the grass with a stiff broom. It is essential that the top dressing is knocked off the blades of grass so that it sifts down to the soil surface.

This thorough working-in prevents the grass from being smothered, and also helps to fill up small hollows.

The benefits of top dressing

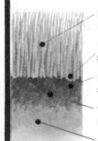

Denser growth of grass. Appearance of new shoots is stimulated.

Minor hollows removed so that a truer surface is obtained.

Damaging effect of alternate freezing and thawing in the winter is reduced.

Water-holding capacity of light soil is improved.

Drainage in heavy soil is improved.

A note on NEAT EDGES

After the first spring mowing, obtain a true edge by using a "half-moon" or a spade, and a wooden plank. Note the sloping cut in the diagram.

Following all subsequent mowings, use the long-handled shears to keep the edges free from overhanging grass. Do not employ the "half-moon" edging iron for this purpose as its continued use will cause the lawn to shrink.

CHAPTER 3
LAWN TROUBLES

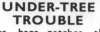

UNDER-TREE TROUBLE
Moss, bare patches, thin stand of grass, see page 24

Black slime on waterlogged turf.
ALGAE
see page 23

Small mounds of earth. Soil sandy: ants present.
ANT-HILLS
see page 24

Small mounds of earth. Soil sticky.
EARTHWORM CASTS
see page 24

NEW-LAWN TROUBLE
see page 35

BROWN PATCHES
see page 26

Brown, leathery, over-lapping "plates".
LICHEN
see page 23

WATERLOGGING
Try spiking (see page 10) followed by sanding. If trouble still not cured, drainage (page 31) is necessary.

STARLINGS and ROOKS
unusually busy—turf torn. Often a sign of
LEATHERJACKETS
see page 26

DAISIES
see page 22

BARE PATCHES
No vegetation present, see page 16

MOSS
see page 23

TOADSTOOLS and "FAIRY RINGS"
(circles of dark-green grass), see page 23

BUMPS & HOLLOWS
For method of removal, see page 16

WEEDS
see pages 18–19

YELLOWISH or PALE GREEN GRASS
covering whole lawn. Most probable cause—nitrogen starvation. Apply Lawn Sand or sulphate of ammonia.

PEARLWORT
(Moss-like but with small white flowers), see page 22

COARSE GRASS WEEDS
see page 22

GRASS THIN and SPARSE
Probable causes—incorrect mowing: page 8
Starvation—feeding needed: page 12
Poor aeration and drainage —spiking needed: page 10
Deep shade: no cure.

"WASHBOARD" EFFECT
Caused by faulty mowing, see page 9

CLOVER
see page 22

BROKEN EDGE
For method of repair, see page 16

LAWN REPAIRS

Bare patches, broken edges, bumps and hollows are all serious troubles. Together they make up th chief cause of the "patchy" effect which spoils so many lawns. With only a little effort, each of thes troubles can be easily cured.

The best time for this repair work is in the autumn. If this is not possible, tackle the job in Apri The weather should be showery to ensure quick recovery.

A note before you begin

Much of this work involves using replacement pieces of turf or the reseeding of small areas. Th grasses making up the turf or seed should be similar to those present in the lawn.

The best source of turf for this purpose is from a section of the lawn where its loss will not b noticeable. The stripped area is then built up with soil and reseeded as described on page 33.

BROKEN EDGES

1
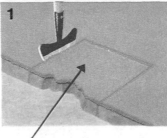

Cut out a square of turf carrying the broken edge.

2
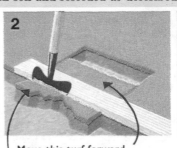

Move this turf forward.

Trim to line up with rest of the lawn.

3

Fill up the gap with eit turf or with soil whic then firmed and sown w grass seed.

BUMPS

Bumps are regularly "shaved" by the mower and therefore tend to become bare. Do not attempt to roll out bumps. This will make the area more unsightly than ever.

HOLLOWS

Hollows carry greener, more luxurious grass than the rest of the lawn. They also drain more slowly in wet weather.

Small hollows can be gradually filled in by working sifted soil (no more than $\frac{1}{2}$ inch thickness at a time) into the soil at regular intervals.

For deep hollows, treat as follows—

1
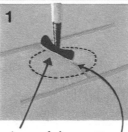

Area of bump or hollow.

Cut turf with spade or edging iron.

2
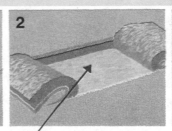

Remove or add soil as necessary to level the turf. Any added soil must be of the same type as the lawn topsoil. New soil should be trodden down.

3

Firm down rolled-back turf

Fill cracks w sifted soil.

BARE PATCHES

Bare patches can be due to a number of causes—

Poor aeration and drainage (spiking needed). Constant drip under trees.

Removal of weeds. The "shaving" of bumps by the mower. Too much traffic, etc. Fertiliser or weedkiller overdose.

Wherever possible, correct the cause before carrying out the repair.

RE-TURFING 1

Remove dead patch of turf and square up affected area. Then break up soil surface with a hand fork.

2

Loosen soil under the new turves with a hand fork. Place them in position.

3

Firm down the turves, and fill in c with sifted soil.

RE-SEEDING

Prick the surface of the affected area with a garden fork. Then rake thorough remove debris and to form a fine seed bed. Firm the surface lightly, and then sow at $1\frac{1}{2}$ oz. per square yard. Cover over with a thin layer of sifted soil and press down a board. Protect the area from birds by means of crossed strands of black thread.

THE PROBLEM OF WEEDS

It is a common sight to see newly sown lawns infested with a wide variety of common garden weeds.

When the lawn is established, however, the introduction of regular mowing brings about a spectacular change in the weed population. Most types cannot stand up to the destructive action of the whirling blades, and so they disappear. Many of the hard-to-kill nuisances of the flower border, such as couch grass, ground elder, bindweed and nettle, are unable to exist in the lawn.

There remains a quite small group with a special low-growing habit which enables them to escape the mower blades. These are the **lawn weeds:**

Rosette weeds

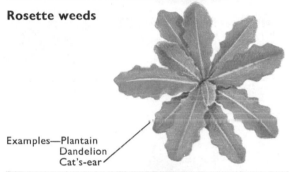

Examples—Plantain
Dandelion
Cat's-ear

Mat weeds

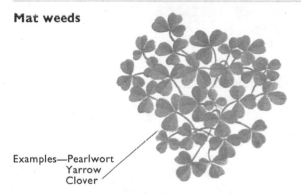

Examples—Pearlwort
Yarrow
Clover

There is nothing you can do to prevent occasional weeds from appearing in even the best cared-for lawn. Wind-borne seeds from neighbouring gardens will see to that.

But Nature cannot be blamed for the existence of large weedy patches all over the turf. The basic reasons for this trouble are

● **poor preparation of the site at lawn-making time**
● **poor choice of turf**
● **neglect**
● **incorrect management**

If your lawn is infested with weeds, you are to blame

HOW TO AVOID THE WEED PROBLEM

1 **When making the lawn, fallow the site before seeding in the autumn.**
Fallowing means the hoeing and raking of the dug but unsown site at fairly frequent intervals throughout the summer. The seeds of annual weeds are induced to germinate and are subsequently destroyed. The weed seedlings must be hoed down before the flowering stage is reached. In this way the danger of the new grass being swamped by a sea of annual weeds is avoided.

2 **When making the lawn, choose good quality seed or turf.**
Buy seed from a reputable supplier. Remember that "bargain" grass seed is often the most expensive in the long run!
Good quality grass seed is carefully checked for purity before sale. There is no doubt that the seedsman is rarely responsible for the weeds which come up with the grass. Improper fallowing is a much more usual cause.
Poor quality turf is more common than low grade seed. Ask to see a sample before purchase.
Turves should be carefully examined and all weeds removed before laying.

3 **On the newly sown or newly planted lawn, hand-weed if necessary.**
This is done by holding down the young grass with one hand and lifting out the weed with the other. Do not use a weedkiller at this stage.

4 **On the established lawn, build up resistance to weeds by good management.**
The cardinal points of correct lawn care are outlined in Chapter 2. If these are followed, the grass will be strong enough to resist a serious invasion by weeds.

5 **On the established lawn, control the occasional invaders by use of a weedkiller.**
"Spot" treatment of individual weeds may be all that is necessary. Where weeds appear to be getting established, an overall treatment is necessary. For full details, see pages 20/21.

COMMON WEEDS

YARROW
MCPA or 2,4-D
2, 4-D + fenoprop
Lawn Sand

DANDELION
MCPA or 2, 4-D
2, 4-D + fenoprop
Lawn Sand

CAT'S EAR
MCPA or 2, 4-D
2, 4-D + fenoprop
Lawn Sand

HAWKBIT
MCPA or 2, 4-D
2, 4-D + fenoprop
Lawn Sand

THISTLE
MCPA or 2,4-D
2, 4-D + fenoprop
Lawn Sand

BULBOUS BUTTERCUP
MCPA or 2, 4-D
2, 4-D + fenoprop
Lawn Sand

CREEPING BUTTERCUP
MCPA or 2, 4-D
2, 4-D + fenoprop
Lawn Sand

CROWFOOT
MCPA or 2, 4-D
2, 4-D + fenoprop
Lawn Sand

WOODRUSH
MCPA or 2, 4-D
2, 4-D + fenoprop
Lawn Sand

RIBWORT
MCPA or 2, 4-D
2, 4-D + fenoprop
Lawn Sand

PLANTAIN
MCPA or 2, 4-D
2, 4-D + fenoprop
Lawn Sand

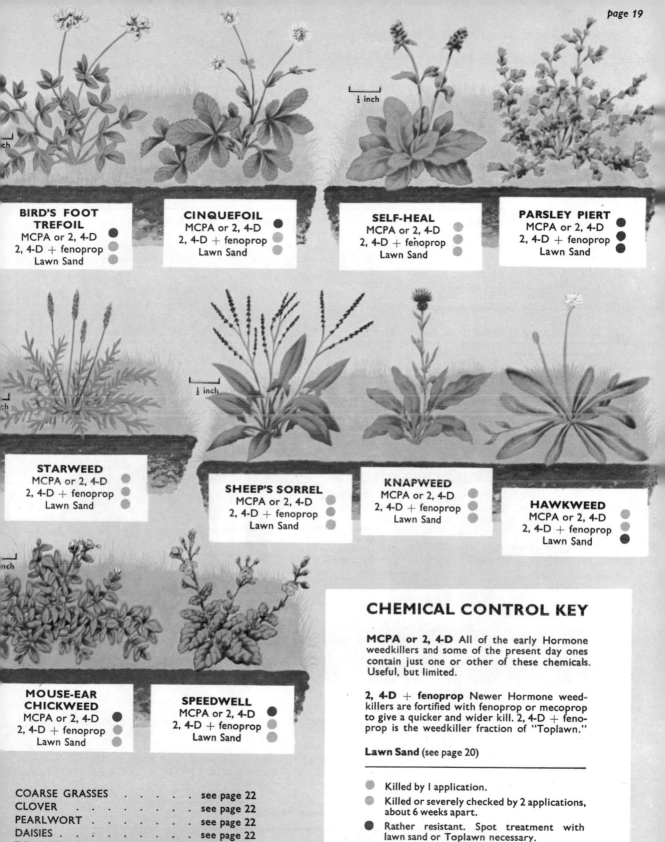

½ inch

BIRD'S FOOT TREFOIL
MCPA or 2, 4-D
2, 4-D + fenoprop
Lawn Sand

CINQUEFOIL
MCPA or 2, 4-D
2, 4-D + fenoprop
Lawn Sand

SELF-HEAL
MCPA or 2, 4-D
2, 4-D + fenoprop
Lawn Sand

PARSLEY PIERT
MCPA or 2, 4-D
2, 4-D + fenoprop
Lawn Sand

½ inch

STARWEED
MCPA or 2, 4-D
2, 4-D + fenoprop
Lawn Sand

SHEEP'S SORREL
MCPA or 2, 4-D
2, 4-D + fenoprop
Lawn Sand

KNAPWEED
MCPA or 2, 4-D
2, 4-D + fenoprop
Lawn Sand

HAWKWEED
MCPA or 2, 4-D
2, 4-D + fenoprop
Lawn Sand

MOUSE-EAR CHICKWEED
MCPA or 2, 4-D
2, 4-D + fenoprop
Lawn Sand

SPEEDWELL
MCPA or 2, 4-D
2, 4-D + fenoprop
Lawn Sand

CHEMICAL CONTROL KEY

MCPA or 2, 4-D All of the early Hormone weedkillers and some of the present day ones contain just one or other of these chemicals. Useful, but limited.

2, 4-D + fenoprop Newer Hormone weedkillers are fortified with fenoprop or mecoprop to give a quicker and wider kill. 2, 4-D + fenoprop is the weedkiller fraction of "Toplawn."

Lawn Sand (see page 20)

- Killed by I application.
- Killed or severely checked by 2 applications, about 6 weeks apart.
- Rather resistant. Spot treatment with lawn sand or Toplawn necessary.

SOLVING THE WEED PROBLEM

If weeds are making your lawn unsightly, then the problem must be tackled as soon as possible with a weedkiller. Delay will mean a steady increase in weed numbers, until the stage is reached when the lawn is beyond repair.

The time to begin is the first recommended period for use for the weedkiller concerned. More than one application may be needed, depending on the weeds present.

After the lawn has been freed from its unwelcome guests, the rules of good management must be followed to increase the vigour of the grass and thereby reduce the chance of re-invasion.

Choosing a weedkiller

LAWN SAND see below	HORMONE WEEDKILLER see page 21	
	Basic types— MCPA and 2,4-D (e.g. Spot)	New wide-spectrum types— fenoprop and mecoprop (e.g. Toplawn)
Use where lawn sand sensitive weeds (see pages 18-19) *and* moss are the problem	Use where plantains, starweed, dandelions and/or buttercups are the problem	Use where clover, daisies, pearlwort or yarrow and basic hormone-sensitive weeds are present

LAWN SAND

Hormone weedkillers have become extremely popular during the past few years, and the older remedy, Lawn Sand, is now often ignored in the weed-control programme. Nevertheless, provided that it is carefully and evenly applied, a single dressing of Lawn Sand will quickly stimulate growth and check a wide variety of weeds.

The way to use it

Sunny morning with the prospect of fine weather.

Grass moist with dew.

4 oz. "Velvas" Lawn Sand per square yard. Even application by hand or distributor is vital. Do not overdose.

Soil must be moist at time of treatment. Do not use during drought.

2 days later: Thoroughly water lawn if rain has not fallen since application.

3 weeks later: Rake up dead undergrowth and apply a further dressing if necessary at 2 oz. per square yard.

How it works

Powder clings to the rough, broad leaves of weeds and coarse grasses. Rapid scorch and leaf destruction results.

Powder slides off the narrow smooth leaves of fine grasses. Temporary blackening of older grass leaves often occurs. Once the powder has been washed down, rapid recovery of grasses takes place.

Powder is washed off leaves on to soil, after which the grass-stimulating and colour-enriching effect occurs.

When to use it

Treatment Period					
APRIL	MAY	JUNE	JULY	AUG.	SEPT.

Best time for treatment

HORMONE WEEDKILLER

A number of weeds, notably plantains, dandelions, buttercups and hawkweed are able to withstand a dressing of Lawn Sand. The discovery of the two Hormone selective weedkillers MCPA and 2, 4-D provided the answer.

Products containing these chemicals have become basic tools for the care of the lawn. Their main blessings are that the killing effect actually takes place **within** the weeds, and a small amount of over-dosing is not liable to scorch the grass.

Nevertheless, from both the efficiency and economy points of view, the maker's recommendations should be strictly followed. Remember that the product cannot distinguish between a weed and garden plant, so store away from plants and avoid drift during application. For liquid weedkillers keep a special watering can or sprayer and wash out thoroughly after use.

The "early" Hormone weedkillers (MCPA and 2,4-D) suffer from two important drawbacks. They are not very effective against a number of important weeds—clover, daisies, pearlwort, etc. Furthermore, they do take a long time to act even on sensitive weeds.

The newer Hormones overcome these drawbacks. Fenoprop acts quickly, and effectively controls the important MCPA-resistant weeds. Mecoprop controls clover.

The way to use it

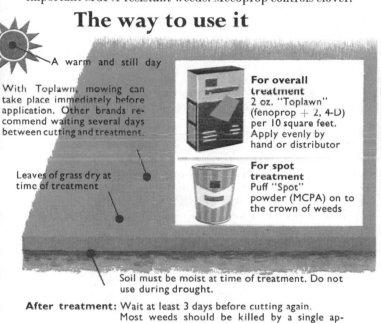

A warm and still day

With Toplawn, mowing can take place immediately before application. Other brands recommend waiting several days between cutting and treatment.

Leaves of grass dry at time of treatment

For overall treatment
2 oz. "Toplawn" (fenoprop + 2, 4-D) per 10 square feet. Apply evenly by hand or distributor

For spot treatment
Puff "Spot" powder (MCPA) on to the crown of weeds

Soil must be moist at time of treatment. Do not use during drought.

After treatment: Wait at least 3 days before cutting again. Most weeds should be killed by a single application. With others a second dressing may be necessary about 6 weeks later.

How it works

The hormone fraction is absorbed by the leaves and rapidly passes to all parts of the weed.
Growth is greatly stimulated at first, and pronounced twisting and curling of the leaves takes place. Finally the weed dies and the leaves rot away.
This will take 2-6 weeks with MCPA or 2, 4-D, but usually only a week or two with fenoprop mixtures.

At the recommended rate of use the amount of weedkiller absorbed by the grass is not enough to do any harm.

When to use it

		Treatment Period			
APRIL	MAY	JUNE	JULY	AUG.	SEPT.

Best time for treatment

Notes on Hormone Weedkillers

NEW LAWNS
Wait twelve months after sowing seed, or six months after laying turf, before applying a Hormone weedkiller.

HOW SAFE ARE THEY?
The word "Hormone" is unfortunate here. They are **not** true hormones and certainly do not have any hormone-like effect on man or animals. They are all harmless to adults and children, pets and wildlife when used as directed.

DISPOSAL OF CLIPPINGS
Lawn clippings obtained shortly after treatment can be used on the compost heap, but this compost should not be used for at least 6 months.
Do not use clippings from freshly treated lawns for mulching around plants.

BULBS IN THE LAWN
Treatment can take place when the leaves of the bulbs have completely withered. Late summer is a good time for this work.

SPECIAL WEED PROBLEMS

PEARLWORT

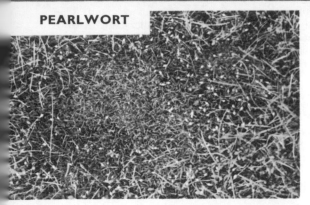

Many weeds are a sign of lawn neglect, but pearlwort often indicates that the lawn has received too much attention. Cutting the grass too close is the usual cause.

Spring raking is a useful start to the control programme. There are two basic chemical control methods. The more effective way is to use a weedkiller containing fenoprop (such as "Toplawn") in late spring or early summer.

The alternative way is to use Velvas Lawn Sand at 4 oz. per square yard.

Pearlwort is often present as large patches before control measures are taken. The use of Lawn Sand will therefore result in extensive bare areas and thin turf. Renovation is necessary, and this involves vigorously raking the area of the dead weeds six weeks after the last treatment, and sowing seed in the seed-bed so created.

CLOVER

Large patches of clover are a sign of nitrogen shortage, or that watering has been neglected during a very dry spell. Once it is well established clover is not easy to remove. The secret is to use a combination of techniques. First of all, rake regularly before mowing so that the creeping stems are brought up to meet the blades.

Water the lawn during drought, otherwise it will spread rapidly.

A chemical attack is also needed and the best answer is to use a preparation containing one of the newer Hormone weedkillers, such as mecoprop or fenoprop. "Toplawn" is ideal and should be used during summer.

A repeat application may be necessary.

Velvas Lawn Sand will effectively burn off the leaves.

COARSE GRASS

The presence of clumps of broad-leaved grasses, such as Yorkshire Fog, Creeping Soft grass, Cocksfoot, etc., will spoil the appearance of any lawn. Luxury-grade lawns are ruined if Perennial Ryegrass secures a foothold.

There is no chemical method of control for these "weed" grasses. If the clumps are scattered and the affected area small, the best way of tackling the problem is to pull out the offending tufts and then fill up the hole with top-soil. This is then re-turfed or re-seeded.

Where hand weeding in this way is not practical, slash the "weed" grasses with a knife or edging iron before mowing. Also rake up the grass before cutting, and change the direction of cut each time you mow.

DAISIES

There may be no objection to a sprinkling of daisies in the utility lawn. But they can get out of hand, and their rapid spread would mean the disappearance of grass from large areas of the lawn.

Daisies are now no longer difficult to kill, as they are sensitive to some of the newer Hormone weedkillers.

Apply "Toplawn" in late or early summer. Repeat the treatment in late summer if a severe infestation is present.

Velvas Lawn Sand will effectively burn off the top growth of daisies.

If daisies are a serious problem, always use a grass-box when mowing until they have been eradicated.

MOSS

This non-flowering tiny plant spreads during autumn and winter when conditions are damp and grass vigour low. Moss is the commonest symptom of run-down turf.

Any one of the causes of poor turf can be responsible for moss invasion. Over-rolling, shortage of fertilisers, poor drainage, the need for spiking, dense shade, over-close mowing, lime shortage and too little top-soil are all common reasons for the spread of this weed.

The only way to ensure permanent freedom from moss is to find the cause and correct the mistake. Note that lime shortage is a *possible* cause but, despite popular opinion, it is by no means the commonest source of trouble. Lime should only be applied when all other factors have been ruled out, and even then a lime-deficiency test should be carried out with PBI Soil Test Paper prior to treatment.

Removal of the cause results in the slow disappearance of moss and the prevention of its return. Eradication can be greatly speeded up by the use of a moss-killing chemical.

Hormone weedkillers must be ruled out because this weed is resistant to their action. On the other hand, "Velvas" Lawn Sand in April at 4 oz. per square yard is very effective. After the moss has been killed by this treatment, rake out the dead material and apply a compound lawn fertiliser (see page 13). Grass seed at 1½ oz. per square yard should be sown to fill up the bare patches.

For eradication in late summer or autumn, use a mercury compound such as P.B.I. Calomel Dust at 1 oz. per square yard.

CHEN

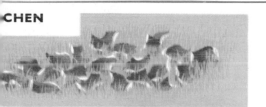

Like moss, the brown leaf-like "plates" of lichen are a symptom of poor growing conditions. Poor drainage, deep shade and food shortage are all common causes.

Eradication is quite simple—the weed is readily killed by "Velvas" Lawn Sand at 4 oz. per square yard. Re-invasion, however, can only be prevented by improving the growing conditions. Spiking, and the application of a compound lawn fertiliser are top-priority operations.

LGAE

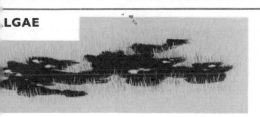

A black slime often coats the surface of waterlogged turf, and is commonly found under the drip-line of trees. The slime is made up of countless microscopic plants (known as blue-green algae), and it can be removed by dressing the affected area with "Velvas" Lawn Sand at 4 oz. per square yard.

To prevent the return of algae, it is necessary to improve drainage either by spiking or, in extreme cases, by the laying of drains (see page 31).

TOADSTOOLS AND FAIRY RINGS

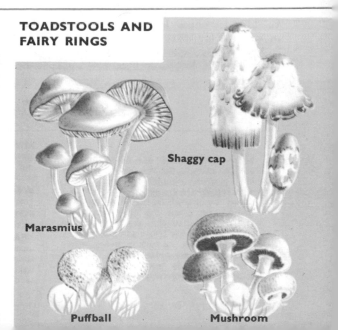

Shaggy cap

Marasmius

Puffball

Mushroom

The toadstools which commonly occur in lawns are not poisonous, and a few scattered here and there over the turf are not particularly objectionable. But, if conditions are right, a rapid spread occurs and a circle containing many toadstools around the edge (a "fairy ring") is produced.

Toadstools are really undesirable when the grass of the fairy ring becomes much darker than the rest of the lawn, so that the area remains clearly visible even when the toadstools are removed. Puffballs are a common cause here. In the most extreme cases the grass in the middle of the dark green ring dies away, so that a narrow band of bare earth results. Rings of this type are nearly always due to *Marasmius*. Chemical control is never easy and is sometimes impossible. The first routine to try is to spike the area of the ring with a garden fork, after which a solution of 2 oz. of Epsom Salts in a gallon of water is applied to each square yard of affected area. If this fails, then try ⅛ oz. of sulphate of iron in a gallon of water per square yard.

If both treatments fail, and the ring is a serious disfigurement, then the only thing to do is remove the turf and top soil from the affected zone and take them well away from the lawn. When all the infected soil has been removed, fill the hole with clean top-soil and re-turf or re-seed the area. Great care must be taken to avoid spilling infected soil on to the healthy surrounding turf during this operation.

WORM CASTS

The case for the earthworm

Earthworms are supposed to have an aerating effect on the soil below the lawn. But this function can be easily improved upon by the garden fork or hollow tine fork.

Scientific research has shown that cast-forming worms produce a waterproof lining to their underground tunnels, so that they do not improve drainage as do ordinary earthworms in the flower bed.

The case against the earthworm

The two cast-forming species of earthworms produce small mounds of sticky earth all over the lawn surface whenever conditions are mild and damp.

These casts are, of course, an eyesore, but even more serious is the direct damage they do to the turf. This is because the structure of the soil making up the cast is quite unlike a good top-dressing. When flattened by feet and the mower, the casts render the surface uneven and stifle the fine grasses they bury. The muddy, slippery surface is then open to weed invasion.

Verdict

Despite the valuable part they play in the vegetable and flower garden, earthworms are a pest in the lawn and they must be eradicated if present in large numbers or deterioration of the surface is certain.

Avoiding the problem

Casts appear in the lawn in spring and autumn, because the mild damp weather brings the active worms close to the surface. The greatest number of casts appear in lawns on loamy or rather heavy soil which is rich in humus. Under these conditions the turf can be rapidly ruined. To reduce the problem, take the following steps—

Do not use lime

Use—Lawn Sand—Garden Peat—sulphate of ammonia—the grass box when mowing.

Curing the problem

A number of wormkillers are available, including Mowrah Meal, Chlordane and Derris. The best time to use these materials is in autumn (September to November) when the weather is mild and showery.

Derris (the worm-killing ingredient in Autumn Toplawn) is completely harmless to pets, birds and children but should be kept away from fishponds. For best results water in immediately after application. Most worms will die in the soil but those which come to the surface should be swept up and removed. Derris is extremely long-lasting and only a single treatment should be required each season.

ANT-HILLS

Unlike worm casts, these small mounds of earth are characteristic of sandy soil lawns and they appear during the heat of the summer.

Ant-hills are not as harmful to the turf as the casts of earthworms, but they do disfigure the lawn, make it uneven and hinder easy mowing.

To kill ants, sprinkle Anti-Ant Powder around the nests. Alternatively, place a few drops of a liquid ant-killer such as Panant close to the hills. This will be carried back to the nest, where the slow-acting poison kills the queen.

A note on TROUBLE UNDER TREES

Shade, food shortage and water shortage are the reasons for the poor growth of lawn grasses under trees.

The trouble is greatest when there is a dense canopy of leaves (for example, beech), or when the tree is shallow rooting so that the grass root zone becomes exhausted (for example, poplar). In these cases, re-turfing every other year may be unavoidable.

The trouble is least when a small-leaved tree is grown (for example, silver birch).

SHADE Thinning out of the branches by pruning will let in more light and so help the grasses. Wood Meadow grass and Rough-Stalked Meadow grass are more shade-tolerant than other lawn grasses.

WATER SHORTAGE Water at the first sign of drought (see page 11).

FOOD SHORTAGE Follow the 3-part Fertiliser plan on page 13.

LEAF DRIP ZONE Trouble is unavoidable in this zone, and very serious in industrial districts. Rake, spike and renovate with seed every autumn.

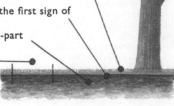

Rake up fallen leaves promptly in the autumn. Do not leave them to stifle the grass below.

THE NEGLECTED LAWN

It is not uncommon to find yourself the owner of a badly neglected lawn. You may have just moved into a house where the garden has been left unattended for some time, or you may have been unable to look after the lawn because of sickness or absence from home. Whatever the cause, the neglected lawn is a depressing collection of overgrown grass and weeds.

Ten point plan to bring it back to normal

1 Carefully examine the grass and weeds covering the lawn. If very coarse grass, moss, pearlwort and other hard-to-kill weeds are dominant, then the best plan is to start again, following the rules for the construction of a new lawn laid down in Chapter 5.

In many cases it will be found that despite the presence of tufts of coarse grass and numerous weeds, the desirable lawn grasses still make up the main part of the lawn. Here, remaking the lawn is not necessary and the best plan is to follow a definite renovation programme, following the rules listed below:

2 Cut down the tall grass and weeds to about a couple of inches from the ground. A billhook or a pair of shears can be used for this job. Only use a scythe if you are skilled in the art! Rake off the cut vegetation. Spring is the best time to begin this renovation programme.

3 Re-examine the lawn surface and, using page 15 as your guide, make a list of the lawn troubles which are obviously present.

4 Rake and brush the surface very thoroughly and vigorously so that dead vegetation and rubbish are removed.

5 Mow for the first time, with the blades set as high as possible. Subsequent mowings should be carried out regularly, as described on pages 8 and 9.

6 Feed and weed the lawn in late spring or summer with a compound dressing such as Toplawn. Apply Calomel Dust if moss is a nuisance.

7 Attack the remaining troubles in autumn by using a combined winter food/wormkiller/fungicide such as Autumn Toplawn.
This will not remove clumps of "weed" grasses which should be dug out.

8 A little later spike the surface, (page 10), **and apply an organic top dressing** (page 13).
If the lawn is thin and open at this stage, mix a little grass seed with the top dressing so that about $\frac{1}{2}$ oz. per square yard is applied.

9 Shortly after spiking and top dressing, carry out all the necessary lawn repairs (see page 16).
Remember to re-seed or re-turf the bare patches left by any weed-killing operations.

10 Beginning in the following spring, the normal lawn management programme can be followed (page 28).

THE PROBLEM OF BROWN PATCHES

Brown patches on the lawn can be due to any of a score of possible causes. It is easy for even the most experienced gardener to make a wrong diagnosis, but with the help of the table below you should be able, with reasonable accuracy, to track down the most probable cause of this trouble in your lawn.

SHAPE OF AFFECTED AREA	COLOUR OF AFFECTED AREA	TIME OF YEAR WHEN IT IS USUALLY SEEN	SPECIAL POINTS OF RECOGNITION	THE KEY QUESTION FOR IDENTIFICATION
Irregular patches or whole lawn affected	Straw-coloured	Late spring or summer		"Did the patches of overall b[r]ing occur after a prolonged p[eriod] of dry weather?"
Small patches 1 inch to 1 foot in diameter	Brown or reddish-brown	Can occur at any time, but autumn is the commonest period for attack	A white mould appears on the surface of the affected area in moist weather	"Does a white mould develo[p] piece of moist affected turf i[n] in a jar for a few days?"
Patches at first small, spreading rapidly to 1 yard or more in diameter	Straw-coloured; often distinctly pink	Late summer or autumn	Tiny thin red needles project from the leaves of dead grass	"Are the patches large and [?] affected grass stems bear red[?] like bodies?"
Patches are small, about 1 to 2 inches in diameter	Brown or straw-coloured	Late summer		"Are the patches small and [?] grass Creeping Red Fescue?"
Small irregular patches which may spread rapidly	Brown	Spring	Birds searching for grubs	"Can the brown grass be [?] pulled away, and are legless grey grubs, about 1 inch in [?] present in the soil?"
Irregular patches, or regular stripes and curves where a fertiliser distributor has been used	Brown or black	Spring or summer		"Was a fertiliser used a few [?] before the discoloration app[?] and was insufficient care p[?] even distribution?"
Small, dead patches	Brown	Any time of the year	A ring of deep green grass surrounds each patch	"Does a bitch have access [?] lawn?"
Irregular patch or patches	Brown	Spring, summer or autumn		"Has the mower been refuel[?] oiled recently whilst standi[?] the lawn?"
Irregular patches	Yellow or brown	Any time of the year		"Were stones, bricks and r[?] not removed from the s[?] soil before seeding or turfi[?] site?"
Irregular patches or whole lawn affected	Yellow or brown	Any time of the year		"Is the top layer of soil comp[?] and has spiking been neglec[?]"

THE TROUBLE MAKERS

DROUGHT

BITCH

SPILT OIL

DISEASE

FERTILISER OVERDOSING

OVER-COMPACTION

BURIED DEBRIS

LEATHERJACKETS

THE ANSWER IS YES, THEN THE MOST PROBABLE CAUSE IS—	AREAS WHERE TROUBLE IS MOST SERIOUS	CURE OR PREVENTION
Drought	Sandy soil areas	The lawn should be watered during dry weather *before* discoloration occurs. If browning has already occurred, spike the surface and water thoroughly.
Fusarium Patch Disease	Commonest lawn disease in all areas	Use "Autumn Toplawn" to prevent disease. Do not use a nitrogen-rich fertiliser in autumn or winter. Spike the turf regularly. If disease has already appeared, treat with a mercury fungicide such as "Verdasan". .
Corticium Disease (also known as Red Thread)	Common in sandy soil areas	Usually a sign of nitrogen shortage. Use "Velvas" Lawn Sand in the spring. Apply a mercury fungicide such as "Verdasan" as soon as the first patches appear.
Dollar Spot Disease	Less common than the other lawn diseases noted above	Use "Autumn Toplawn" to prevent disease. If disease has already appeared, treat with a mercury fungicide such as "Verdasan".
Leatherjackets (grubs of Daddy Longlegs)	Damage is worst on light soil and coastal areas	Apply "Soilicide" in late autumn at the rate of $\frac{1}{2}$ oz per square yard. Rake into the turf and lightly water in.
Overdosing with Fertiliser		Follow the maker's instructions when applying fertiliser or Lawn Sand.
Bitch Urine		Water the affected areas copiously. This will reduce but not eradicate the discoloration.
Spilt Oil		Always move the mower off the lawn before oiling or refuelling.
Buried Debris		Lift back turf, remove offending object and then resoil and replace turf.
Over-compaction	Heavy soil areas	Spike every autumn, and introduce a drainage system (see page 31) if waterlogging still occurs.

CHAPTER 4

LAWN CALENDAR

APRIL

Feeding and weeding can begin towards the end of the month, provided that the grass and weeds are actively growing. A dressing of "Toplawn" at 2 oz. per 10 square feet will feed and green the turf for months and also kill weeds quickly.

If moss is a problem use "Velvas" Lawn Sand and rake up the dead moss a fortnight later.

Mow often enough to stop the grass growing away, but do not cut lower than three-quarters of an inch.

Dig out patches of coarse grass or resistant weed. Fill the holes with sifted soil and then re-seed or re-turf.

JANUARY

There is very little work to do on the established lawn this month, apart from brushing away fallen leaves.

Walking on the turf in January may cause a certain amount of harm if the surface is waterlogged or frozen.

This is a good time to have the mower overhauled.

MAY

Continue mowing, increase the frequency as necessary and lower the height of cut closer to the summer level (see page 8). Once a week mowing starts in May.

In most seasons this is the best month for weed-killing with either a Hormone preparation or Lawn Sand (see pages 18-22 for guidance on picking the right chemical and formulation for your purpose). Remember the need for dry grass, moist soil and a fine day when using a weedkiller.

If drought threatens now or during the later months, apply water early and copiously as instructed on page 11.

FEBRUARY

In mild districts the lawn care season may begin this month, with the appearance of worm casts. If these are very numerous they should be brushed off and a wormkiller applied.

Do not be tempted into cutting your lawn before March arrives.

JUNE

Summer mowing should now be under way. Twice a week cutting will be necessary when the soil is moist, but if there is a long dry spell raise the height of the cut and leave off the grass-box. If you decide to water the grass, really soak it.

Another "Toplawn" dressing or Lawn Sand treatment should be carried out if any appreciable quantity of weeds have managed to survive the first treatment. Use "Spot" application for isolated weeds.

Raking before mowing is important this month as the combined action keeps the runners of clover under control.

If the lawn has not been fed so far and a quick green-up is required, apply "Lawn Tonic" or sulphate of ammonia.

MARCH

The yearly lawn work programme really starts this month. As soon as the grass has started to grow and the weather and ground conditions are suitable, brush the lawn vigorously with a birch broom to remove the surface rubbish which might otherwise damage the roller.

Next, roll when the surface is dry to consolidate any pockets which have been lifted by frost. Follow this with a thorough raking with a wire rake, so that the weeds and grass are set up to meet the mower blades.

The first cut should merely "top" the grass; close cutting at this stage could result in severe yellowing or browning. Two cuts are generally sufficient this month. Neaten the edges with a half-moon edging iron.

JULY

Mow regularly at the summer height, water if dry weather is prolonged and rake occasionally as recommended for June.

If Clover, Pearlwort, Yarrow and/or Mouse-ear Chickweed suddenly appear as serious problems, apply Fenoprop + 2, 4-D (see page 21).

AUGUST

The same general treatment as for July. Try to make lawn-cutting arrangements in your absence if your holiday is to be a long one.

Use "Spot" treatment on scattered weeds if necessary.

SEPTEMBER

The autumn programme begins this month with the increasing interval between mowings and the raising of the height of cut to the autumn level, which is a quarter of an inch above the summer cutting height (see page 8).

Worms may become active at this time; use "Autumn Toplawn" which will effectively control worms which make casts, prevent Fusarium and Dollar Spot diseases, and also feed the grass roots during the rest of the autumn and winter. Carry out lawn repairs during showery weather at the middle or end of the month. Bumps, hollows, broken edges and bare patches can be rectified by following the instructions on page 16.

If moles are a nuisance, tackle the problem now by gassing them with Topvil fuses.

This month and next month is the ideal time for spiking (after a thorough raking) and top-dressing.

If disease patches have already appeared, use a mercurial fungicide (see pages 26-27).

OCTOBER

Regular mowing comes to an end during October. For the last cut or two, set the cutting cylinder high and the edges should be trimmed for the winter.

Apply "Autumn Toplawn", carry out lawn repairs, spike and top-dress if these jobs were not carried out last month.

Brush up leaves, which would harm the grass and increase the worm problem if left on the surface.

Dig out tufts of coarse grass and re-seed or re-turf.

For the new lawn, seed sowing should be completed at once, but the ideal turfing season is only just beginning.

NOVEMBER

If weather is "open" (not frosty or wet) and the surface firm, mow once with the blades set high during the month.

It is not too late for worm killing, if casts continue to appear.

Keep the turf free from leaves.

DECEMBER

Apart from brushing away leaves, December is the slack end to a busy year.

Keep off the lawn if it is very wet or frozen.

THE NEW LAWN

The grass in your new lawn can come from either seed, turf or planted sprigs. Each of these methods has its good and bad points.

The choice between them may have to be made only once in the life of your garden. So consider the respective merits and drawbacks carefully before coming to a decision.

	SEED	TURF	PLANTED SPRIGS OF CREEPING BENT
Approximate cost per 100 square yards	£3 5 0 (Luxury grade mixture) £2 5 0 (Utility grade mixture)	£11 10 0 (Standard turf) £32 10 0 (Cumberland turf)	£6 0 0
Advantages	Seed sowing is the most inexpensive method of lawn production. In addition, you can obtain a mixture which is tailor-made to suit your particular conditions. Providing that you specify exactly what you want from a reliable supplier, you are sure of obtaining the correct grasses with a guaranteed purity and germination capacity. Seed does not quickly deteriorate after purchase so you can wait for a few days or even weeks for suitable sowing weather without harm.	Turfing is the quickest method of lawn production. In a matter of a few weeks a vigorous and mature-looking lawn is obtained, ready for use and immune to seedling troubles such as "damping-off" and birds. Summer fallowing (see page 32) and the production of a fine seed bed are not essential prior to turfing, but they are important pre-requisites for sowing and seed planting sprigs. Turf is laid in late autumn or winter, the slackest period of the gardener's year.	Planting sprigs of Creeping Bent is the newest method of lawn production. If the Grower's instructions are carefully followed, the sprigs quickly root and spread to form a close carpet of fine-leaved matted grass. Spring planting can produce a mature lawn in autumn if conditions are good. It is claimed that "planted" lawns require less mowing and weeding than sown or turfed ones. Every time the edges of the lawn are cut, fresh planting material is obtained free of charge.
Disadvantages	A period of 9–12 months must elapse after sowing before the new lawn is ready for use. Grass seedlings are delicate and are liable to damage by birds, bad weather and "damping-off". The preparation of the soil bed must be very thorough.	Much of the turf offered for sale contains a high proportion of coarse grass and numerous weeds and weed seeds. Turf suitable for luxury grade lawns is extremely difficult to obtain. Turf has to be laid as soon as possible after delivery, but the recommended time for turf laying is often the worst time for getting on to the land.	Planting is a much more laborious job than seed sowing, and it must take place within a day or two of receiving the sprigs. Creeping Bent is shallow rooting, and the turf it produces is not considered suitable for really hard wear. Raking or incorrect mowing can drag up the grass mat.
Planting or sowing time	Best: Mid-August to mid-September Next best: April	Best: October to February Next best: March to April	Best: Autumn or early spring
In a nutshell ...	1½ oz. seed spread evenly 3 feet 3 feet Lightly rake in seed after sowing	Note bonding of turves Standard turf Cumberland turf 3 feet 3 feet Brush sand or sandy loam into cracks after laying	3 feet 3 feet soil sprig of Creeping Bent soil
For further details	See page 33	See page 34	See Grower's leaflet

PREPARING THE SITE

Step 1 Get down to bare earth

SUMMER
TUMN if level-
is not required.

The first job is to clear away bricks, rubble, rubbish and piles of subsoil left by the builder.
Next, strip off the top inch of soil and remove it from the site. These sods of rough grass and weeds
should be inverted at a suitable spot and rotted down with the help of an activator such as Bio
Compost Maker. The compost will be ready for use in about 12 months.

Step 2 Grade the site *(Omit this step if levelling is not required)*

SUMMER

The purpose of grading is to change the contours of the site so that the approximate final level is
obtained.
Basic Rule: Remove the top-soil and stack it at a convenient point. Make all the necessary
alterations with the subsoil. When the desired level has been obtained, replace the top-soil. On no account should subsoil be
brought to the surface. If the top-soil layer is less than 6 inches thick, then buy a load or two from a local supplier.

Obtaining a level surface:

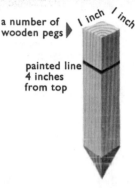

a number of
wooden pegs ▶   1 inch 1 inch

painted line
4 inches
from top

one
straight-edge
board
7 feet long

one
spirit
level
about
1 foot
long

1 Set the pegs to the desired level

6 feet

6 feet

2 Add or remove soil
from between the pegs
until the soil surface is
level with the painted
line on each peg.

Grading a sloping site:

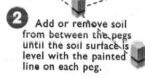

top-soil

subsoil

top-soil removed ----- A

subsoil

Soil A is moved to its new
position in 6-inch layers.

Tread down each layer before
adding the next.
Do this treading when the soil
is reasonably dry.

top-soil replaced

A

subsoil

Step 3 Drain the site *(Omit this step if the site is free-draining)*

SUMMER
TUMN if level-
is not required.

If the soil is heavy and the drainage is naturally poor, some form of drainage system is essential,
otherwise the new lawn will rapidly deteriorate.
If levelling is undertaken—put in the drainage system when *Grading* (Step 2)
If levelling is not undertaken—put in the drainage system when *Digging* (Step 4)

Drainage systems:

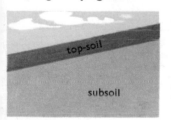

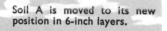

1½ feet   1½ feet

2 feet

inches of top-soil

inches of small
ones, clinker etc.

inches of hard
ore, large stones,
roken bricks etc.

he easiest method
to build one or
ore "soakaways"
the lowest part of
e lawn.

2
A more efficient
method is to spread
a 4 to 6 inch layer of
broken bricks,
clinker etc. on top
of the subsoil when
grading or digging.
Press well down,
cover with ashes,
and then replace the
top-soil.

3 Very few gardens warrant the costly and
elaborate system of tile drainage, but it
is without doubt the best method.

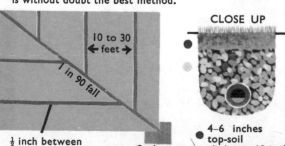

10 to 30
◀ feet ▶

1 in 90 fall

½ inch between
drainpipes

Soakaway

CLOSE UP

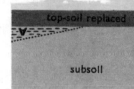

4-6 inches
top-soil
clinker and 3-inch
drainpipe

PREPARING THE SITE

Step 4 Dig the site

AUTUMN

This should be done with either a fork, spade or mechanical cultivator to a depth of about 9 inches, or less if the top-soil is shallow. Do not bring up subsoil if less than 6 inches of top-soil is present, then buy a load or two to make good the deficiency. Depending on the soil type, the addition of sand or humus-making material may be necessary at this stage.

Heavy soil
Work in about 14 lb. coarse lime-free sand per square yard when digging.

If subsoil is clay, fork over the bottom of the trench to the full depth of the prongs.

Light soil
Work in about 7 lb. Irish Peat, compost or well-rotted manure per square yard when digging.

Remove large stones and roots of perennial weeds as the work proceeds.

Step 5 Break down the soil clods

SPRING if site is to be sown

AUTUMN if site is to be turfed

The easiest way of doing this is to trample the roughly dug earth with your feet. Use a strong iron rake to remove debris and stones, and then trample again.

An alternative method of consolidation is to slowly roll the site when the soil is dry, rake, and then roll the surface again.
If the clods left after digging are *not* properly broken down before preparing the surface for seed sowing or turf laying, later settlement will produce an uneven lawn.

Step 6 Prepare the soil bed

ONE OR TWO WEEKS LATER

This involves raking the consolidated ground to produce a reasonably fine stone-free tilth in the top inch or two of the top-soil.
After raking, re-tread the site by walking on your heels so that soft spots are revealed.
Rake again, to remove the bumps and hollows and to produce the necessary fine crumb structure.
Repeat the treading or rolling operation followed by raking until the soil bed is firm enough not to settle nor show heel marks, but still soft enough to have a crumb structure.
Check the final level.
The site is now ready for turfing. Where seed is to be sown, go on to Step 7.

Step 7 Fallow the site

MAY to AUGUST

The purpose of fallowing is to get rid of the dormant weed seeds in the soil. This involves raking and hoeing at about monthly intervals during the summer. This treatment promotes weed seed germination, and the weed seedlings are destroyed by the next hoeing. Tread or roll the surface between hoeings.

Step 8 Complete the soil bed

AUGUST to SEPTEMBER

Check the level. A final raking should produce a firm seed bed. The aim is not to have a soil particle in the top inch which is larger than a grain of wheat.
The site is now ready for sowing.

SOWING SEED

To reach the stage of the final seed bed takes a lot of patience and hard work.

In contrast, seed sowing is a simple and straightforward task. But carelessness at this stage can undo all of the hard work which has gone before.

1 Before sowing

In order to give the grass seedlings a flying start, apply 2 oz. of P.B.I. Growmore Fertiliser per square yard to the seed bed about a week before the proposed sowing date. Lightly rake into the surface.

2 Sowing the seed

The best time to choose is between mid-August and mid-September, when the soil is still warm and the weed and water shortage problem is reduced to a minimum.

April sowing is often successful, but watering will be necessary if the summer is dry.

Buy sufficient seed mixture to allow an application rate of 1½ oz. per square yard. Lower rates may mean a delay in the production of an established lawn; higher rates will increase the risk of "damping-off" (see page 35).

Pick a day when the surface is dry but the soil below is moist. The weather should be fine and calm. Gently rake the surface soil in straight lines so that very shallow furrows are produced.

Next, thoroughly shake the bag of seed and divide it into 4 equal parts. Uniformly distribute the quarters by hand as follows:

¼ of the seed down the lawn

¼ of the seed left to right

¼ of the seed right to left

¼ of the seed up the lawn

In this way the errors of distribution and the chance of missed patches are reduced. Instead of broadcasting the seed by hand, a distributor can be used, sowing half the seed across and the other half up and down the site.

3 After sowing

Lightly rake the whole area with a wire rake so as to partly cover the seed. Rolling is not recommended, as it is liable to cake the surface.

If birds are likely to be a nuisance, criss-cross strands of black thread 3 or 4 inches above the ground to keep them away.

Seed mixtures

The damage caused by a poor seed mixture cannot be easily undone. It is the types of grass present, and not the attractiveness of the trade name which counts.

Avoid mixtures which contain a large number of different species as patchy results are often obtained.

There is no such thing as the perfect seed mixture. The best seed mixture for your purpose depends upon the use to which the lawn will be put, the soil type and aspect of the site, and the price you are prepared to pay.

LUXURY GRADE MIXTURE
7 parts Chewings Fescue
3 parts Browntop Bent

UTILITY GRADE MIXTURE
4 parts Chewings Fescue
3 parts Perennial Ryegrass
2 parts Crested Dog's Tail
1 part Rough-Stalked Meadow grass

SHADE TOLERANT MIXTURE
5 parts Rough-Stalked Meadow grass
3 parts Wood Meadow grass
2 parts Creeping Red Fescue

4 Appearance of the seedlings

Time of sowing	Time taken for shoots to appear
Autumn	1–2 weeks
Spring	2–3 weeks

When the seedlings are 1–1½ inches high

Gently sweep off worm casts and leaves on a day when the surface is dry. Follow this by a light rolling with the back roller of the mower. This treatment encourages the seedlings to produce new shoots, and it firms the soil lifted by the germinating grass.

When the seedlings are 2 inches high

The new lawn is now ready for its first cut. The blades must be set high (at least 1 inch from the fixed bottom blade) and they must be sharp. In this way the grass is merely "topped".

Mowing should be carried out at regular but not too frequent intervals to keep the grass under control. Gradually bring down the blades to the height recommended on page 12.

5 Removing the weeds

Use the technique illustrated on page 17.

6 Watering the new lawn

This is essential if a dry spell occurs after sowing. The need for sprinkling is much more likely with a spring-sown lawn than with an autumn one.

LAYING TURF

The disadvantages of turf compared with seed as a method of producing a new lawn are both obvious and important.

Good turves are very expensive and hard to find, and you can never be sure of getting just the grasses you want.

But turfing has an attraction which to many gardeners outweighs all of the disadvantages—the bare soil bed is transformed into a "finished lawn" in the span of a few hours.

1 Before laying the turf

About a week before the proposed laying date, apply 2 oz. of P.B.I. Growmore Fertiliser per square yard to the soil bed, which has been prepared by the technique described on pages 31 and 32.

Lightly rake the fertiliser into the soil.

2 Getting the turf ready

Standard turves (3 feet × 1 foot) will be rolled up when delivered to you.

STACKING
If they are to be laid within 24 hours

If laying is to be delayed—

Choose a shady spot, water if necessary

Buying turf

The farmer's idea of good grass is almost completely opposed to the needs of the lawn owner. For this reason **turf taken from pastures and meadows** is not suitable for anything more than a rough utility grade of lawn.

Best of all is **parkland turf**, stripped from a site close to your own home. Failing this, aim for **downland turf**, which is also made up almost entirely of fine-leaved lawn grasses.

Unless you are already a lawn expert, **Cumberland turf** is best avoided. Although it is made up of Creeping Fescue and Bent, it nearly always rapidly deteriorates when used for inland lawns.

The most important rule when buying turf—ask to see a sample first. Remember that isolated weeds can easily be removed, but to change the type of grass present is a long or even impossible job.

BOXING

This is an essential step if the turves are of different thicknesses.

excess soil trimmed off

knife fitted with 2 handles

Turf placed grass side down in open-ended wooden box made from pieces of board.

INSPECTING Before each turf is placed in position, the surface should be inspected and weeds pulled out. If a lot of coarse grass is present, reject the piece of turf and place on the compost heap.

3 Laying the turf

RIGHT WAY Standing on a plank laid across the turf

Start along one side of the site. Work in straight lir Note bonding the turves, bricks ir w

Press the turves closely together

WRONG WAY Standing on prepared soil bed

If a hollow is present, make good with sifted soil.
If a mound is present, cut it away before the turf is placed finally in position. Do not attempt to beat it down.

The best time for turf laying is between October and February.
Spring turfing is possible, but you must water regularly to prevent the turves dying and shrinking along the joints.

4 After laying the turf

Spread a mixture of sand and sifted soil along the cracks and work this dressing into the turves with a broom or the back of a rake.
Follow this a few days later with a light rolling.

5 Spring treatment

"Top" the grass when it begins to grow in the spring. The blades should be gradually lowered until the recommended height of cut (see page 8) is reached.
Feeding (page 13) and top dressing (page 14) will help the new lawn to become rapidly established.

TROUBLES IN THE NEW LAWN

YOUNG GRASS THIN AND SPARSE. COMPLETE GREEN CARPET NOT FORMED

Possible causes:

1 Seeding rate too low—Use 1½ oz. per square yard.

2 Poor site preparation—the mistakes usually responsible are insufficient attention paid to drainage and the presence of subsoil in the surface layer.

CRACKS BETWEEN TURVES

Watering has been neglected during dry weather.

ANNUAL WEEDS

If these are numerous enough to be a problem, it indicates that fallowing (page 32) has not been carried out.

YOUNG GRASS SLOW-GROWING AND PALE

It is sometimes found that the young grass turns pale green and almost ceases to grow.

If this happens in the spring, a stimulant containing nitrogen is required to give it leaf-making vitality.

A very dilute liquid fertiliser should be applied through a fine-rose watering can. Be careful to cause as little seedling and soil disturbance as possible.

The application rate for Bio Plant Food is 1 teaspoonful in 1 gallon of water to 4 square yards.

BUMPS & HOLLOWS

The soil was not properly consolidated after digging.

GERMINATION PATCHY OR GENERALLY POOR

Possible causes:

1 Poor preparation of the site—Patchiness is often due to areas of subsoil which have been brought up to the surface by the faulty cultivation of the soil.
2 Poor weather conditions—Both dry spells in light land areas and prolonged wet periods on heavy land are frequent causes of this trouble.
3 Birds
4 Old seed
5 Uneven sowing
6 Disease—"Seed Rot" kills the grass seed before the emergence of the seedling. This trouble is worst when the soil is not free-draining, when the seed is old and the weather cold and damp.

Treating the seed with a thiram seed dressing is a useful preventive.

PATCHES OF YELLOW OR BROWN SEEDLINGS

If seedlings have toppled over:

1 Disease—"Damping-off" is the cause here, and it is easily recognised by the blackened area which occurs at the base of each affected seedling. The leaves turn brown or reddish-brown.

The Bents are more susceptible than other lawn grasses.

"Damping-off" is most likely to occur where seed has been sown too thickly and when the weather is humid.

As soon as patches of the disease are seen, water the whole area with 1 oz. of Cheshunt Compound in 2 gallons of water to every 2 square yards of lawn.

If the seedlings have not toppled over:

2 Poor preparation of the site—Buried bricks and rubble are a frequent cause of discoloured patches in newly-sown lawns.

3 Poor weather or soil conditions—Both dryness and waterlogging of the surface inch of seed bed can cause the yellowing and subsequent death of grass seedlings.

Renovating a newly-sown lawn

The thin areas and bare patches should be raked, taking care not to alter the level of the surface. Use the same seed as sown previously, and mix one part of seed with 10 parts of sifted sandy soil. Spread this evenly over the raked areas at the rate of ¾ lb. per square yard. Lightly rake the seed in after sowing.

Printed in Great Britain by Jarrold & Sons Ltd., Norwich.

PUBLISHED BY PAN BRITANNICA INDUSTRIES LTD.
WALTHAM CROSS, HERTS, ENGLAND.